The
Mirror,
the Window,
and the
Wall

The Mirror,
the Window,
and the Wall

THE LIFE-CHANGING POWER OF FINDING YOUR TRUE SELF

KENNY G. DOWN

New Thought Life

NEW THOUGHT LIFE, LLC
Seattle, WA

Printed in the United States of America

First printing 2021

Paperback ISBN: 978-1-7356628-2-4
Hardcover ISBN: 978-1-7356628-5-5
eBook ISBN: 978-1-7356628-3-1

NEW THOUGHT LIFE, LLC
Seattle, WA

NewThoughtLife.org

I dedicate this book to Darlene

Narkiewicz, a woman who found her

True Self and showed many more how to

awaken to their authentic purpose in life.

She continues to inspire us all.

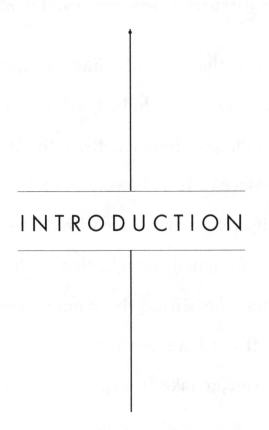

INTRODUCTION

The most important question you can ask yourself is whether or not you were born with an innate need to find the spiritual way of life. You might ask: how can I tell? Well, if you feel at times beaten and crushed under the pressure of life, this may be a good sign.

The idea that we must find the spiritual life in order to quit hiding, to find our True Self, and, most importantly, to live is not a new concept. It is, however, one I wish to solidify, refine, and share with others. This was the original thought that pushed me to write The Mirror, the Window, and the Wall. If you have ever felt the pull toward the divine, to take on a spiritual quest, this booklet may speak to you.

There are those also who are able to live with an obscured view of themselves through a lens they attempt to control, to focus so that others view them in a certain

·

way. They get away with building walls to protect themselves and hide behind. Those who can live with this are numerous; this booklet may also be for them if they desire a better quality of life. Everything that pushes us towards spirituality does not have to be life or death.

The mirror, window, and wall are metaphors for all those tactics we use to hide the lie that we believe is the truth: the false self. Each of these elements are the persona, the mask. Here, ancient Rome comes to our aid. The persona, or personality as we now say, was originally used in ancient

Rome and referred to the masks the actors of the day would wear to represent the various characters. Like the ancient Romans, we may be wearing a mask, playing a character, reading a script assigned to us.

My point in writing this booklet was not only to show how we put the mask on ourselves but how, through those societal pressures and false beliefs, the mask is placed on us imprinted with others' DNA. The mask we wear may have the fingerprints of those other than ourselves.

·

"You should appear like this to be attractive to society." Hearing this often enough, seeing this in media and advertising, we absorb these unconscious beliefs about ourselves. When we have been told or hear in some way the message that we are never "good enough" it becomes our mantra. A capitalistic view of success is also thrust upon us simply by being born where and when we are born. This supplants the honest desire we came into this life with: to be a helpful cocreator with God.*

This booklet is intentionally brief; however, its meaning is deep-seated and profound. It may even appear hidden on the first read. Therefore, this is a book that is meant to be read over and over.

I propose you incorporate your reading with the following seven actions. These are suggestive only; however, like most desirable things in life, the more time you put into it, the more spiritual understanding you gain, the closer you will be to taking the first steps on a newfound Spiritual Quest.

·

1.) Read through every day for a week.

2.) Read aloud to hear your own voice saying the words.

3.) Read at the same time and the same place each day.

4.) Meditate, in contemplative fashion, each day on what you read.

5.) Write one paragraph each day on what came to you in meditation.

6.) Recite Darlene's Prayer** before and after you read each day. Repeat several times throughout the day.

7.) Partner up. Share your reflections with a friend, or a group who has completed the same practice.

My hope as the author is that you, the reader, will begin the discovery of your True Self or, if you are already on this path, that you will continue expanding this awareness.

I have chosen in this writing to use the feminine pronouns of she/her for the main character; however, these lessons are universal and apply to all individuals, regardless of their experience or gender identification. Our paths are all unique. The shape and materials used to build our mirrors, windows, and walls may differ. The opportunity to see our own True Self is universal and available to all readers.

·

The term God, when used in this book, does not refer to any one religion and, in fact, includes them all. It can be whatever you, the reader, are most comfortable envisioning. This is always to be taken as your own concept of a Power greater than yourself. It should only be defined by what it means to you.

**Darlene's Prayer can be found at the end of this booklet.*

THE MIRROR

"If they knew the truth, they wouldn't love me, they'd shun me, hurt me, abuse me, laugh at me." We have said this to ourselves so many times that we live in this false narrative.

·

The mirror is how she saw herself. This reflection was neither the truth, nor near the truth. It was designed by the false self. She didn't see her True Self, but a reflection of what others had told her she should be. She saw ugliness where there was beauty.

She saw disappointment where there was bright future. She saw expectations where she should have seen encouragement. She saw brokenness where there was wholeness. She saw emptiness where there was Spirit. The list went on, turning into a lifelong, devoted, laborious project to shield herself from her own fears, projected failures, and lack of control in life. She wasn't born with the mirror in her hand, but she had held it as long as she could remember and didn't recall picking it up.

The mirror was created not in reality but in her own lost world, a world of spiritual darkness, a world of make-believe. She was spiritually asleep, physically awake, hiding from the bogeyman. The mirror reflects what she had painted on its surface over many years. She gazed into a distorted image, manifesting a self-centered view of the world and its people.

Like her, the mirror in our hand, that we once occasionally looked at, slowly becomes a wrap-around, three-hundred-and-sixty-degree mirror. After years of self-delusion, we don't realize that we are viewing the world in a dream state. We see only how every life event reflects on our image. We

·

become lost in a false world with our ego-centric view as the only reality we know. We believe we are looking at the world, but we are only able to see the world as it reflects on us. We see the world through the stories we make up about ourselves and those told to us by others. Some of the stories we believe, some are just easier to tell than what we believe is the truth, more bearable. "If they knew the truth, they wouldn't love me, they'd shun me, hurt me, abuse me, laugh at me." We have said this to ourselves so many times that we live in this false narrative.

·

She stuffed the truth into the darkest place she knew, somewhere deep within. She pretended it wasn't there. Hard work was this. She was exhausted. She was temperamental, unavailable, and erratic. She blamed everyone she could, "you'd be this way too ... if you had my life." Somewhere within her own inner consciousness she knew she was profoundly wounded, genuinely lost. She was the victim, the perpetrator, and the witness to the crime.

She believed the wraparound mirror was the world. It was not. When she saw her truth, it reminded her that it was long overdue to shatter the mirror, open her eyes, and awaken to truth. The mirror was shattered for her when her resources failed her, when circumstances of living this way of life crushed her to earth. She took a monumental fall, the mirror shattered; no amount of self-will could restore her image. There are no words to describe where she had been, none. Those who have held the mirror know. Those who have suffered, as she has, know.

THE WINDOW

The window becomes our stage in life. We alone control the curtains, the sound, the lights. We play a role assigned to us that has nothing to do with who we really are.

The window is the only vantage point she allowed her fellow travelers to view her from. To protect herself, the window was designed in intricate detail and multilayered form. It was a window that she controlled and manipulated to show only

•

what she wanted the world to see. She showed and highlighted only her best features. She cracked the window only enough so others could listen to what she wanted them to hear. The real thoughts—her inner "thought life," the steady, never-ending thoughts that flowed through her mind— were never allowed to be heard. All this filtering to defend the persona . . . no wonder she ended up spiritually broken, lonely, fear-filled, and ashamed. The window was a distorted lens. What the window allowed to be seen and heard was neither the truth nor near the truth.

Similarly, she viewed the world through this window, seeing what she thought was the reaction of others to her presence. She read into situations explanations derived from her own wrong thinking. "They must be talking about me," "they are laughing at me," "they don't like me." With this view of the world who wouldn't feel compelled to attempt the impossible, to somehow take control of others' viewpoints and opinions of them?

But there never was any real control, only the illusion that she controlled the focus, that she alone controlled the window of what other people could and could not see and hear. Hard work was this. She tried to control all of this while pretending to be at ease with herself. And if the facade briefly faltered and fell away, her hands perceivably shook, her face twitched, her heart raced, and her breathing became shallow and rapid. Signs of exhaustion from keeping up this level of dishonesty were now taking its toll. It became clear to all that something was wrong. No matter how great the distortion on the window was, no matter how far closed it became, it was no longer fooling anyone. She knew she was in real trouble. She was overwhelmed.

Like her, we do not want others to see us as we think we are. Believing the lie, we think we are who we see in the mirror, so we put up the window. We may try to play the role of the genius, the good-looking or lovable hero. We may portray ourselves as the champion, the egotist, or the proverbial know-it-all. When that doesn't work, we begin to play the worst of the worst, allowing those looking through the window to only see the bravado and hear the foul language we use; surely this would keep anyone from getting too close. We are critical and condemning in judgements we project onto anyone who tries to be friends.

We play the victim, the sufferer, the sick. Either way we are actors, sometimes wittingly and sometimes so far asleep we don't even know we are playing a role. The window becomes our stage in life. We alone control the curtains, the sound, the lights. We play a role assigned to us that has nothing to do with who we really are. If we are given the gift of intelligence, athletic ability, business savvy, or wealth, then we latch onto that role and use this as justification to feel more superior than our fellows, fueling our self-centeredness even more.

·

For her, the truth was revealed to herself and others when the mirror was shattered and the window opened. She was, in that moment, naked and bare, stripped of her false self. The spiritual awakening began with the smashing of the mirror and the opening of the window. For her, it was done against her will.

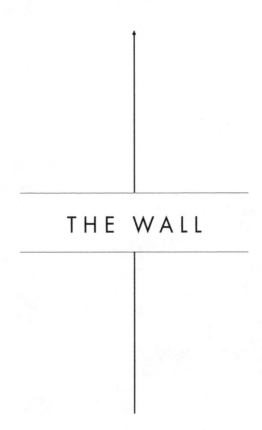

THE WALL

It was remarkable that she built the wall and yet believed it was others who were laying the bricks.

When the window opened and all could see around and over, nobody believed her lies anymore. The brave ones looked into her eyes and offered a solution. This was when she began to build the wall. One brick at a time, higher and higher

•

she went. It was somewhere in her child-hood that she laid the first row. She didn't remember exactly when; she only knew she could never stop.

She felt lonely, even in a crowd who gen-uinely loved her. She felt alone when she was praised; she self-destructed when crit-icized. She believed she knew the truth about herself. "They're only being kind to me to appear nice, they really don't like me." One day turned into a week, a week turned into a month, and soon years had gone by and she was walled in from all sides.

She was convinced that what separated her was that she had been victimized, shunned, and thrown away. It was remarkable that she built the wall and yet believed it was others who were laying the bricks. It was then that she screamed, "Somebody please help me!" She thought nobody heard.

Her body broke down, she began to seek treatment for one syndrome after another, her greatest symptoms exhaustion and fatigue. Like her, even in our sleeping hours our minds are hard at work keeping all the pieces of the mirror, the window, and the wall in place.

•

She climbed to the top of the wall to peer over; she stumbled and fell. She felt like she had been pushed; some say she jumped. With the mirror shattered, the window opened wide, and the wall now behind her, she had nowhere left to hide. She was broken and couldn't run. She lay sprawled on the ground, face down to earth. Falling off the wall did not come willingly. It was by divine intervention when all else had failed—her failure was to become her freedom. And so, it was with us. Whether she was forced by nature's winds, had been internally spooked and stumbled, or had reached the end and jumped. Whichever way, God had shoved her.

THE TRUE SELF

Once she had awakened, a wonderful healing gift came to her. Not only did she see herself as God saw her, but she was given the gift to see others as they are!

W e awaken to the Truth in one of two ways. The lucky ones decide to face the genuineness of their situation and seek a deeper, spiritual life. They are willing to leave behind all falsehoods they have so laboriously set up and do so for a new and infinitely better life. For others, they are beaten beyond recognition or words and are wheeled in on a gurney. She was brought to God on a stretcher.

For her, there was only one answer when she arrived; she had tried everything else. She asked for divine life support. She prayed for help and it came. Through a committed, unrelenting, devoted, and inspired dive into the spiritual life, she was to find Love for herself. She was brought to a place of acceptance, to this truism. She could finally see the truth: that neither the window, the mirror, nor the wall were her True Self. It was neither the truth nor near the truth. *Who was she then?* There was no more important question to be asked. So, it was with her, *Who am I?* Or better yet, *What am I? Why do I accept a role assigned to me against my will? If I lose the assigned role what will become of me?*

As she gained spiritual understanding and committed to healing, she was able to drop the role she had played for so many years. Only then did she begin to find her True Self. It was not comfortable, this period between shedding her false persona and finding her genuine, authentic self. It was

a difficult, terrifying, vulnerable, and anx-
iety-riddled process. She trudged ahead;
it remained as the only friendly direction.
She knew to shrink would mean disaster.

Never could she return to the mirror, the
window, or the wall; those were tools that
no longer worked. They had protected her
for many years, shielded her from painful memories, prevented her from further
exposure to cruelty. They had worked . . .
until they didn't.

Rising within her was the knowledge that
she was born with: seeking spiritual help

was her only hope. She was not learning anything new; she was remembering what she once knew and had long ago forgot. The knowledge that she was an innately spiritual being rang with the truth of ancient wisdom. Being stripped of the false self was a painful process and the spiritual life came in as a cool, soothing, healing balm.

Placed deep in her soul was the intuitive compass, the mystical road map to where she needed to go. She found spiritual community; she sought out spiritual teachers, those that had been on this path and succeeded. She read spiritual books and built an altar. She prayed and practiced meditation. Slowly all those things that were not her fell away. What was left was a loving child of God, her True Self. She was the Bodhisattva.

For her, it was there all along and nothing ever changed that. For all of us, we are the loving children of God. We are the heirs to all of God's creation. We are a part of, and inseparable from God. This discovery is the bedrock under the foundation, the underpinning of the spiritual experience found by followers of any spiritual culture, fellowship, or religion. This is the

THE TRUE SELF

•

most important unearthing forevermore.

This is why the exploration of inner space

outweighs any discovery we will ever make

traveling to the far reaches of outer space.

When she made this discovery, had this

realization, she laughed more, loved more,

worried less. She was healthier, happier,

and whole. She was free!

Once she had awakened, healing gifts

came to her. Not only did she see herself as

God saw her, but she was given the gift to

see others as they are! Her third eye, what

Westerners sometimes call the sixth sense,

was opened. Intuition came. In a way no

one who had not been through this trans-formation could, she was able to look at the walled-in person and know that they were only playing a role. She could see through the lightly veiled attempt to protect their own false self and see the True Self long before it was apparent to anyone else. She saw them as they were, her true family in the spiritual life, with an inborn spiritual core. They were as she was, the Buddha, the Christ, the Prophet, the Mother, the Father, the Child. One of seven billion brothers, sisters, and friends on this planet.

For her, hopelessness preceded willingness. Willingness led her to the Truth. The Truth was Health, Happiness, Wisdom, Love, Humility, Intuition, and Intelligence. The mirror, the window, and the wall are distant memories for her now. She has found and learned to maintain her True Self, she has awakened, she knows. This was spiritual understanding not of the intellect, but of the soul. It is who she is.

·

DARLENE'S PRAYER

Lord of the Happy, Joyous, and Free,

*I grant you permission to repair
the broken mirror.*

*I pray now that I would see the
reflection of my True Self,*

So Strong and Beautiful and Free.

*I grant you permission to open
the window wide,*

*That others may see me for
who I really am.*

*I pray now that they really see me,
and I them,*

So Love-filled, Honest, and Kind.

*I grant you my permission to
tear down the wall.*

*I pray now that you would take away
all I use to build barriers.*

I am so tired of hiding.

*I commit with your helping hand
to step into the sunlight,*

*To Shine, Illuminate, and Empower
myself and others.*

Amen

ABOUT THE AUTHOR

Author Kenny Down lives in Seattle, WA. His other works include *Darko: The Sacred Heart of One Johanee Darko*, *Awakened Giant Sleeping Spirit*, and *The Care and Keeping of a Shan*, as well as an array of poetry, short stories, blogs, and vlogs.

Kenny can be reached through his website *NewThoughtLife.org*.